flutter

fly

scary

# The Usb
# First
# Illustrated
# Thesaurus

noisy

loud

### Jane Bingham
### and Caroline Young

Illustrated by
Tjarda Borsboom
and Beatrice Tinarelli

bang
bang!

gigantic

massive

Edited by
Felicity Brooks

Designed by
Kirsty Tizzard

speed

zoom

# Using this book

A thesaurus is a book that groups together words with the same or similar meanings. You can use it to find words to make your writing and speaking more interesting. So you can change this:

My friends are nice. We went to a nice party and had a nice time.

to this:

My friends are lovely. We went to a fantastic party and had a wonderful time.

This thesaurus is divided into topics. You can search through the book to find a topic you want, or check the contents on pages 4 and 5.

Look at the words and pictures to give you ideas.

Find a range of words to make your writing more varied.

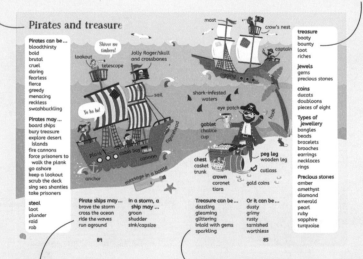

Discover striking phrases.

Choose from a list of interesting words to describe things.

# Using the word finder

If you want to find other ways to say a particular word, use the word finder on pages 96 to 104. It is in alphabetical order, so to find the word 'nice', look under 'n'.

The word finder will help you choose a word.

**nervous**, 18

**nice**, 6

**noise**, 81

The word finder tells you to look on page 6 to find other words that mean 'nice'.

# Choosing words

Each time you write or speak, you make choices about words. Here are some ways to use words to create dramatic effects.

Make people come to life by showing how they look, sound and act.

The pirate had <u>flowing hair</u> and a <u>menacing grin</u>. He gave an <u>evil cackle</u> as he <u>waved</u> his hook.

Describe how places look, sound, feel, and even smell.

Parrots <u>screeched</u> in the <u>dark</u>, <u>steamy</u> jungle, and the air was filled with the <u>scent</u> of flowers.

Create a sense of speed and movement by using lots of action words.

The spaceship <u>zoomed</u> through the clouds, <u>hurtled</u> past the planet and <u>raced</u> away.

# Contents

soar

swoop

fast

quick

hurry

rush

colourful

bright

jolly

happy

content

stroll

walk

# Good, bad, nice

**A good artist**
expert
gifted
skilful
talented

**A good child**
angelic
obedient
polite
well-behaved

**A good book**
brilliant
excellent
marvellous
wonderful

**A bad person**
cruel
evil
nasty
wicked

**Bad behaviour**
cheeky
disobedient
mischievous
naughty

**A bad smell**
disgusting
horrible
revolting
vile

**A nice time**
amazing
fantastic
great
wonderful

**A nice view**
beautiful
breathtaking
spectacular
stunning

**A nice person**
helpful
kind
lovely
warm-hearted

# Big and small

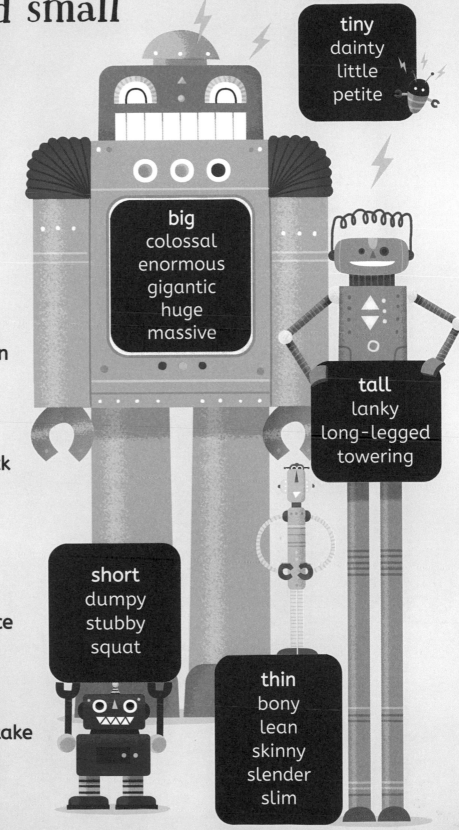

**A big person**
beefy
fat
heavy
hefty
large
overweight

**A big lake**
immense
vast
wide

**A big decision**
important
major
serious

**A small speck**
microscopic
minute
teeny
tiny
titchy

**A small space**
cramped
narrow
poky

**A small mistake**
minor
slight
unimportant

**tiny**
dainty
little
petite

**big**
colossal
enormous
gigantic
huge
massive

**tall**
lanky
long-legged
towering

**short**
dumpy
stubby
squat

**thin**
bony
lean
skinny
slender
slim

# Colours

**Colours can be ...**

**dark**
deep

**light**
pale

**bright**
bold
brilliant
fluorescent
garish
luminous
rich
vivid

**dull**
dingy
drab
dreary
faded
faint
muddy

**More colours**
beige
black
brown
cream
fawn
hazel
ivory
khaki

**yellow**
lemon
mustard

**red**
crimson
ruby
scarlet

**white**

**grey**
charcoal
dove grey

**pink**
coral
rose pink
salmon pink

**blue**
navy
royal blue
sky blue
turquoise

**orange**
amber
apricot
peach

**green**
bottle green
emerald green
lime green
olive green

**violet**
lavender
lilac
mauve

**purple**
maroon
plum

# Shapes and patterns

**Shapes can be ...**
hexagonal
rectangular
square
triangular

**round**
circular
globular
spherical

**flat**
level
smooth

**pointed**
sharp
spiky

**long**
stretched-out

**short**
squat

## Flat shapes

circle

square

edge/side

triangle

oval

diamond

rectangle

pentagon

hexagon

octagon

## Solid shapes

corner    point

sphere    cone

cube      pyramid

**Patterns can be ...**
bold
delicate
eye-catching
floral
flowing
random
regular
swirling

stripes

checks

zigzags          spots/polka dots          spirals

9

# Describing faces

**Faces can be ...**
heart-shaped
long
round

**good-looking**
attractive
beautiful
handsome
pretty

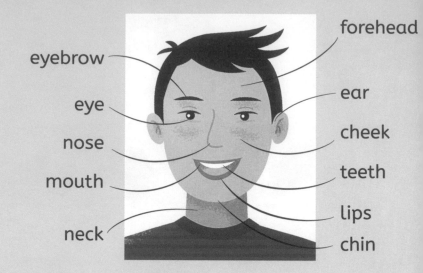

forehead
eyebrow
eye
nose
mouth
neck
ear
cheek
teeth
lips
chin

## Faces can have ...

glasses

wrinkles · freckles · a beard · braces

stubble · spots · a moustache · dimples

## People may ...

grin · smile · frown · blush

# Hair and hairstyles

## Hair can be...
curly
floppy
flowing
frizzy
greasy
lank
receding
shiny
sleek
spiky
straggly
straight
windswept
wiry

**thick**
bushy
shaggy

**thin**
fine
thinning
wispy

## Hair may be...
bleached
dyed
gelled
layered
permed
scraped back
shaved
spiked
tinted

## Hair colours
auburn
black
blonde
brown
chestnut
fair
ginger
grey
mousy
red
silver
white

## Hairstyles
bob
bunches
crew cut
dreadlocks
mohican
ponytail
pudding bowl
quiff
ringlets
short back
  and sides
top knot

## Other hair words
bald patch
hairband
hair clip
hair extension
hair slide
sideburns
wig

bun
fringe
parting
plait
pigtail
cornrows
tangled
wavy
braids

11

# Clothes and shoes

wool

pleats

vest

raincoat

T-shirt

tights

sweater/
jumper

skirt

## Coats
anorak
cagoule
duffle coat
parka

## Hats
baseball cap
beanie
beret
bobble hat
sunhat
top hat

## Dresses
pinafore dress
sari
tunic

## Trousers
jogging bottoms
leggings
shorts

## Underwear
boxer shorts
bra
knickers
pants
underpants

## Tops
cardigan
fleece
hoodie
shirt
sweatshirt

## Nightclothes
dressing gown
nightdress/
   nightie
pyjamas
slippers

## Other clothes
braces
gloves
mittens
onesie
scarf
socks
suit
tie
tracksuit
waistcoat

## Shoes and boots

canvas

flip-flops

sandals

pumps

wellingtons

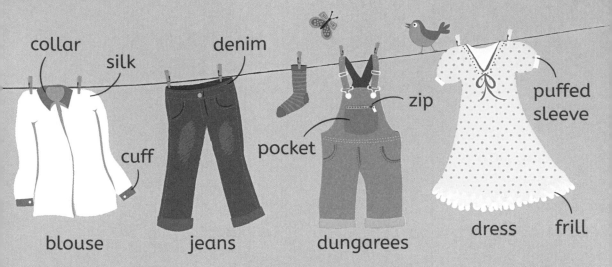

**collar**
**silk**
**cuff**
blouse

**denim**
jeans

**pocket**
**zip**
dungarees

**puffed sleeve**
dress
**frill**

## Clothes can be made from ...
corduroy
cotton
fur
lace
satin
velvet

## Some clothes have ...
buttons
fringes
patches
ruffles
sequins
tassels

## Clothes can be ...

**smart**
neat
tidy

**scruffy**
frayed
shabby
ragged

**tight**
clingy

**loose**
baggy

**flowing**
floating

**dirty**
grubby
muddy
stained

**They can also be ...**
comfortable
elegant
fancy
fashionable
fun
itchy
plain
sporty
trendy

**shoelaces**

**leather**

walking boots

trainers

slippers

shoes

# Talking and thinking

**Let's have a talk**
chat
conversation
discussion
gossip
heart-to-heart

**Please talk quietly**
keep your voice
  down
talk softly
whisper

**Don't talk so loudly**
bawl
bellow
raise your voice
shout
yell

**I think it's too late**
believe
expect
feel
guess
imagine
reckon
suppose

**Let's think about what to do**
chew over
concentrate on
consider
contemplate
decide
focus on
weigh up
work out

**I think you're wrong**
believe
consider
reckon

**We must think up a plan**
come up with
create
dream up
invent

**Amy likes to sit and think**
brood
dream
imagine
ponder
reflect
wonder

**Other words for 'say'...**

**announce**
declare
state

**answer**
reply
respond

**ask**
beg
demand
enquire
question

**mention**
comment
point out

**mutter**
mumble
murmur

# Action words

**walk**
hike
march
plod
saunter
stagger
stomp
stride
stroll
trek
trudge
wander

**climb**
clamber
scale
scramble

**jump**
bound
hurdle
leap
spring

**push**
drive
force
press
prod
ram
shove

**pull**
drag
heave
tow
tug
yank

**take**
grab
help yourself
pick
seize
select
snatch

**give**
deliver
hand over
pass
present

**hold**
clasp
cling on to
clutch
grab
grasp
grip
hang on to
seize

**carry**
lift
lug
move
shift
transport

**put**
dump
lay
leave
place
plonk
rest
set
stand

**squash**
crumple
crush
flatten
squeeze

**sit**
perch
rest
sprawl
squat

run

race

dash

gallop

sprint

hurtle

15

# All sorts of feelings

I'm feeling ...

weary

energetic

delighted

uneasy

proud

**angry**
cross
fuming
furious
irate
livid
seething

**bored**
fed-up
restless

**confused**
baffled
bewildered
dazed
flummoxed
muddled
puzzled

**surprised**
amazed
astonished
shocked
startled
stunned

**happy**
cheerful
chirpy
glad
overjoyed
over the moon

**excited**
eager
keen
thrilled
wound up

**worried**
anxious
distressed
fretful
on edge
tense
troubled

**sad**
depressed
devastated
down in the
  dumps
heartbroken
low
miserable
tearful
unhappy
wretched

contented

nervous

confident

flustered

## Love and hate

**I love ...**
adore
am devoted to
am in love with
am very fond of
think the world of

**I hate ...**
can't bear
can't stand
despise
detest
loathe

**tired**
exhausted
shattered
sleepy
worn out

**grumpy**
annoyed
bad-tempered
cranky
cross
grouchy
irritable
peeved

**upset**
distressed
hurt
shaken

**scared**
afraid
frightened
panic-stricken
petrified
scared stiff
startled
terrified

**When you're
angry, you ...**
clench your fists
grind your teeth
scream
shout
slam doors
stamp your foot
yell

**When you're
sad, you cry**
burst into floods
of tears
shed tears
snivel
sob
wail
weep
whimper

**When you're happy,
you smile**
beam
grin
grin from ear
to ear
smirk

17

# All kinds of people

**People can be ...**

**young**
babyish
childish
youthful

**old**
aged
ancient
elderly

**strong**
athletic
hefty
muscular
strapping

**weak**
delicate
feeble
helpless
puny

**healthy**
fine
fit
in good shape
well

**cheerful**
cheery
chirpy
happy
jolly
light-hearted
optimistic

**calm**
easy-going
laid-back
peaceful
relaxed

**nervous**
jittery
jumpy
on edge
tense

**crazy**
daft
foolish
idiotic
insane
mad
silly

**honest**
trustworthy
truthful

**dishonest**
deceitful
two-faced

**polite**
courteous
well behaved

**rude**
bad-mannered
cheeky
impolite

**unkind**
cruel
mean
nasty
spiteful

**kind**
caring
generous
helpful
warm-hearted

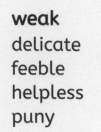

**brave**
bold
courageous
daring
fearless
plucky

**clever**
brainy
bright
gifted
intelligent
knowledgeable
smart
talented
wise

**clumsy**
awkward
bumbling
butter-fingered

**funny**
amusing
comical
hilarious
ridiculous
witty

**fussy**
choosy
hard-to-please
pernickety
picky

**lively**
bouncy
bubbly
chatty
confident
energetic
full of life
high-spirited

**naughty**
badly behaved
cheeky
disobedient
mischievous
wild

**nosy**
curious
inquisitive
interfering
prying
snooping

**proud**
arrogant
boastful
conceited
haughty
high and mighty
snobbish
snooty
stuck-up
uppity
vain

**sensible**
down-to-earth
level-headed
practical
wise

**shy**
bashful
quiet
self-conscious
timid

**confident**
calm
fearless
poised

# Your body

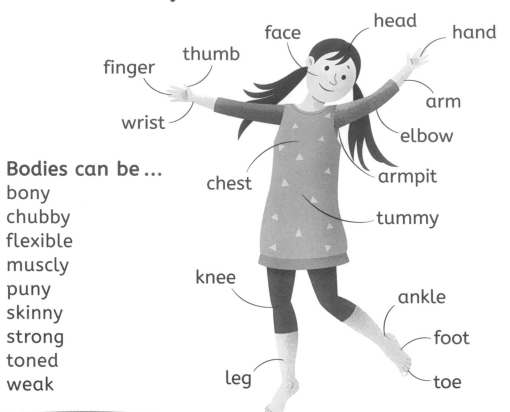

face
head
hand
thumb
finger
wrist
arm
elbow
armpit
chest
tummy
knee
ankle
foot
leg
toe

**Bodies can be ...**
bony
chubby
flexible
muscly
puny
skinny
strong
toned
weak

# Inside your body

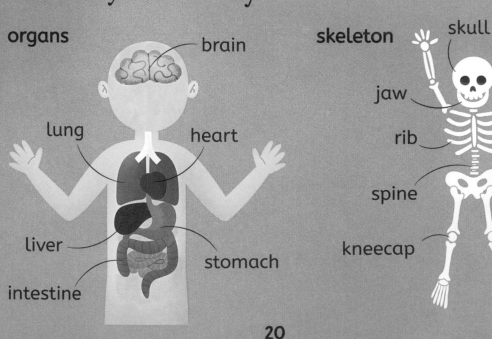

**organs**

brain
lung
heart
liver
stomach
intestine

**skeleton**

skull
jaw
rib
hip
spine
kneecap

# Your senses

**I can smell roses.**
scent
sense
sniff out
track down

**Smell this perfume.**
breathe in
inhale
sniff

**Taste this treat.**
nibble
sample
sip
try

**Can you taste lime in this dish?**
make out
notice
recognize

*chirp chirp!*

**Did you hear that noise?**
catch
notice
pick up

**Please listen!**
concentrate
pay attention
prick up your ears
take in

**Did you see that star?**
catch sight of
notice
spot

**Please don't look.**
gaze
peep
peer
watch

**You won't feel any pain.**
be aware of
experience
notice

**Feel this scarf.**
handle
run your hands over
touch

# Feeling ill

## I've got a...

bruise

cut

headache

lump

rash

tummy ache

temperature

toothache

## Are you...?

coughing

shivering

atishoo!

sneezing

itching

**I'm feeling...**
awful
bad
faint
poorly
shaky
sick
unwell

**You could have...**
an allergy
a broken bone
a bug
a cold
a disease
an infection
a virus

**Or you could have...**
asthma
chickenpox
hay fever
flu
measles
mumps

# Getting better

**Hospital words**
accident and
    emergency
clinic
operating theatre
ward

**You may need ...**
an appointment
an examination
an injection
an operation
a prescription
an x-ray

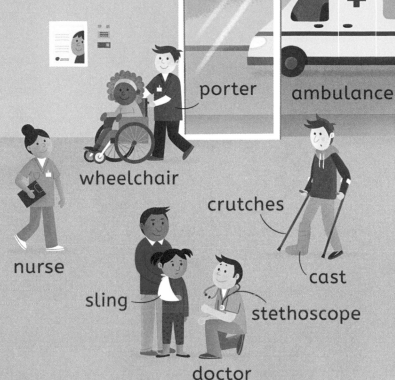

porter

ambulance

wheelchair

crutches

cast

nurse

sling

stethoscope

doctor

## In a medicine cabinet ...

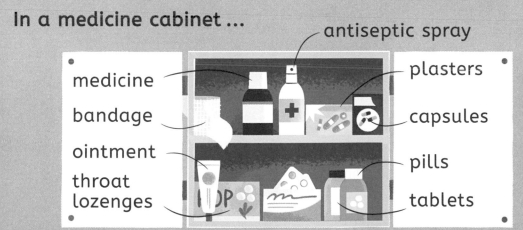

antiseptic spray

medicine

plasters

bandage

capsules

ointment

pills

throat
lozenges

tablets

**We need to look
    after Jess.**
care for
cure
nurse
take care of

**Then she'll
    get better.**
get well
heal
improve
recover

**Now she's
    feeling fine.**
all right
better
fit
healthy

# Food and drink

melon  pineapple
pear
grapes
orange
plum
bunch of
bananas

**Food can taste ...**
bitter
bland
fresh
mouldy
rich
salty
sour
stale
sweet

**Food can feel ...**
chewy
creamy
greasy
juicy
lumpy
rubbery
slimy
stringy

**soft**
gooey
mushy
sloppy
soggy
spongy
squishy

**hard**
crisp
crunchy
tough

**Fruit**
apple
cherries
grapes
lemon
lime
peach
strawberries

**Fish**
cod
haddock
mackerel
plaice
salmon
sardines
tuna

**Seafood**
crab
lobster
mussels
oysters
prawns
scallops
shrimp

FISH FILLETS

SHELLFISH

**Meat**
bacon
duck
gammon
goose

ham
kidney
lamb
liver

offal
salami
steak
turkey

PORK CHOPS

CHICKEN DRUMSTICKS

SPICY SAUSAGES

MINCED BEEF

## In a salad you may find ...
avocado
beetroot
celery
cucumber
lettuce
peppers
spring onions
tomatoes

## Vegetables
aubergine
broad beans
cabbage
cauliflower
leeks
mushrooms
peas
runner beans
spinach

chillies    garlic

sweetcorn

onions

carrots    broccoli

potatoes

## Takeaway food
burger
chips
curry
ice cream
noodles
pasta
pizza
sandwich

## Bread and cakes
bagel
bread roll
brownie
bun
cupcake
doughnut
flapjack
muffin
naan
pitta

SLICED LOAF

## Dairy foods
butter
cheese
cottage cheese
cream
goat's cheese
margarine
milk
sour cream
yogurt

MILK

## Drinks
coffee
juice
lemonade
milk shake
smoothie
squash
tea
water

## Drinks can be ...
**fizzy**
sparkling

**refreshing**
thirst-quenching

**warm**
lukewarm
tepid

**cold**
chilled
freezing cold
ice-cold

**hot**
boiling hot
piping hot
scalding

# Eating and drinking

**eat**
bite
chew
gnaw
gobble
munch
nibble

**drink**
gulp
slurp
suck

**You eat quickly**
fast
hurriedly
rapidly
swiftly

**I eat slowly**
carefully
steadily

**Food can be ...**
**delicious**
mouthwatering
scrumptious
tasty
yummy

**disgusting**
foul
revolting
vile

I'm thirsty

I'm hungry

Yuck!

jug

glass

fork

knife

plate

mustard

ketchup

cup

spoon

mug

pie dish

## How much food?

a crumb

a bite

a slice

a spoonful

a bowlful

a piece

a plateful

# In the kitchen

grater

hood

scales

saucepan

frying pan

sieve  colander  ladle  toaster

fridge

sink

freezer

spatula

apron

mixing bowl

recipe

cutter

blender

rolling pin

chopping board

casserole dish

whisk

wooden spoon

baking tray

## Ways to prepare food

| | |
|---|---|
| beat | stir |
| blend | whip |
| grate | |
| knead | **chop** |
| mash | cut up |
| mix | dice |
| peel | slice |

## Ways to cook food

| | |
|---|---|
| bake | poach |
| barbecue | roast |
| boil | simmer |
| deep-fry | steam |
| fry | stew |
| grill | stir-fry |
| microwave | toast |

# Inside a home

tiled roof

chimney

attic/loft

drainpipe

bedroom

double bed

bathroom

shower

bedside table

staircase/ stairs

sitting room/living room/lounge

study

desk

balcony

garage

kitchen

front door

dining room

**In the kitchen**
cooker/oven/stove
cupboard/cabinet
dishwasher
kettle
microwave oven
mixer
sink
tumble dryer
washing machine

**On the floor**
carpet
floorboards
tiles
rugs

**On the walls**
paint
tiles
wallpaper

**Types of furniture**
armchair
bookcase
bunk bed
chest of drawers
dining table
rocking chair
single bed
sofa/couch
wardrobe

# Homes and gardens

**Homes can feel**
airy
cosy
cramped
damp
dark
draughty
dusty
homely
luxurious
roomy
spacious
stuffy
welcoming

**This house is ...**

**messy**
cluttered
untidy

**tidy**
neat
well-organized

**clean**
immaculate
polished
scrubbed
spick-and-span

**Different homes**
apartment
bungalow
cottage
detached house
farmhouse
flat
houseboat
log cabin
mansion
mobile home
palace
semidetached
  house

**In a garden**
fishpond
flowerbed
paddling pool
path
patio
swimming pool

**Gardens can be ...**
blooming
colourful
neglected
overgrown
overrun by weeds
well kept

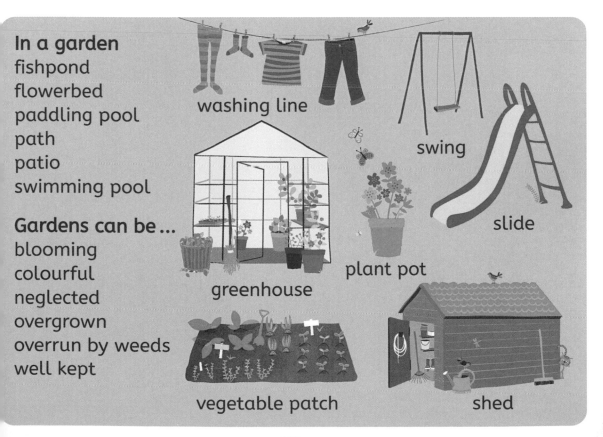

washing line

swing

slide

greenhouse

plant pot

vegetable patch

shed

# Building words

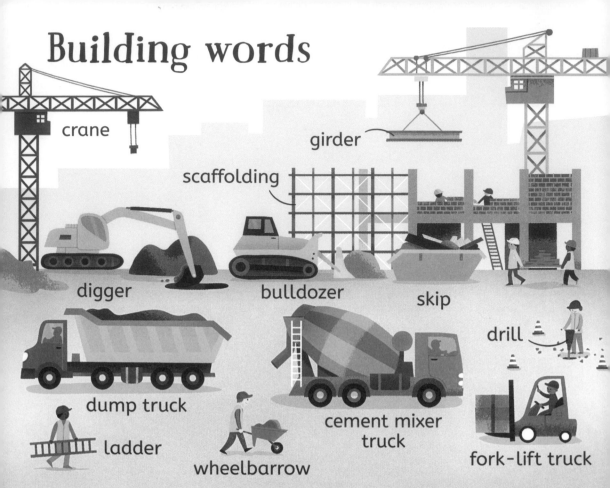

crane

girder

scaffolding

digger

bulldozer

skip

drill

dump truck

ladder

wheelbarrow

cement mixer truck

fork-lift truck

**build**
construct
erect
put up

**People on site**
architect
builder
electrician
labourer
plasterer
plumber
site manager

**Vehicles and machinery**
excavator
front loader
pneumatic drill
rock breaker

**Buildings can be made from ...**
brick
concrete
steel
timber

**On a building site you can hear ...**
banging
crashing
hammering
sawing
shouting
shovelling
thumping

hard hat

cement

trowel

bricklayer

# Tools and materials

nuts

bolt

## Materials can be ...

**soft**
springy
squashy

**hard**
firm
rigid
solid
stiff

**strong**
sturdy
tough

**weak**
brittle
flimsy
fragile

clear
see-through
transparent

**smooth**
glossy
polished
silky
sleek

## Different materials
glass
leather
metal
paper
plastic
rubber
stone
wood

## Types of metal
aluminium
brass
bronze
copper
gold
iron
lead
silver
steel
tin

## Types of wood
ash
beech
cedar
ebony
mahogany
oak
pine

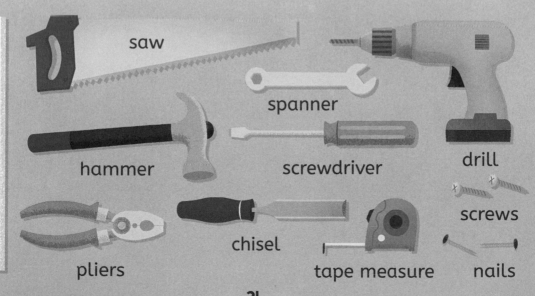

spirit level

saw

spanner

hammer

screwdriver

drill

chisel

pliers

tape measure

screws

nails

# In a city

**Cities can be ...**

**busy**
bustling
buzzing
crowded
exciting
lively
noisy
packed

**dirty**
grimy
polluted
smoggy
smoky

**empty**
deserted
echoing
eerie

**shabby**
run-down
scruffy

**shiny**
gleaming
glittering
sparkling

hotel

cathedral

high-rise flats

library

theatre

cinema

restaurant

coffee shop

shopper

commuter

busker

window cleaner

office block

billboard

**City buildings can be ...**
futuristic
grand
imposing
impressive
stunning

shopping centre

mosque

college

flower stall

art gallery

museum

bank

road sweeper

subway

human statue

tourist

newspaper seller

tour guide

33

# Going shopping

greengrocer  barber  bookshop  pet shop  florist

toyshop  clothes shop  butcher  newsagent

cash machine

bank  hairdresser  post office  shoe shop  bakery

| store | cheap | money | | |
|---|---|---|---|---|
| department store | inexpensive | cash | card | coins |
| megastore | reasonable | change | | |
| superstore | reduced | payment | | note |

# At a supermarket

BUY ONE, GET ONE FREE

That's a good deal.

freezer

groceries

carton

bottles

That's too expensive.

chiller

trolley

scales

FRUIT & VEG

customer    assistant

basket

aisle

shopping list

salad bar

fish counter

deli counter

SELF-SERVICE MACHINES

queue

PLEASE PAY HERE

cashier

till

reusable bag

checkout

carrier bag

35

# On the road

**Vehicles may ...**
accelerate
brake
break down
collide
crash
crawl
cruise
race
skid
slow down
speed up
squeal to a halt
swerve
veer

_toot!_

_zoom!_

bus

bus stop

sports car

motorhome

pedestrian
crossing

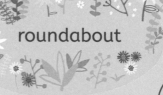

roundabout

road sign

camper van

fire engine

**Cars can be ...**
dented
gleaming
rusty
streamlined

steering wheel

windscreen

bonnet

boot

headlight

tyre

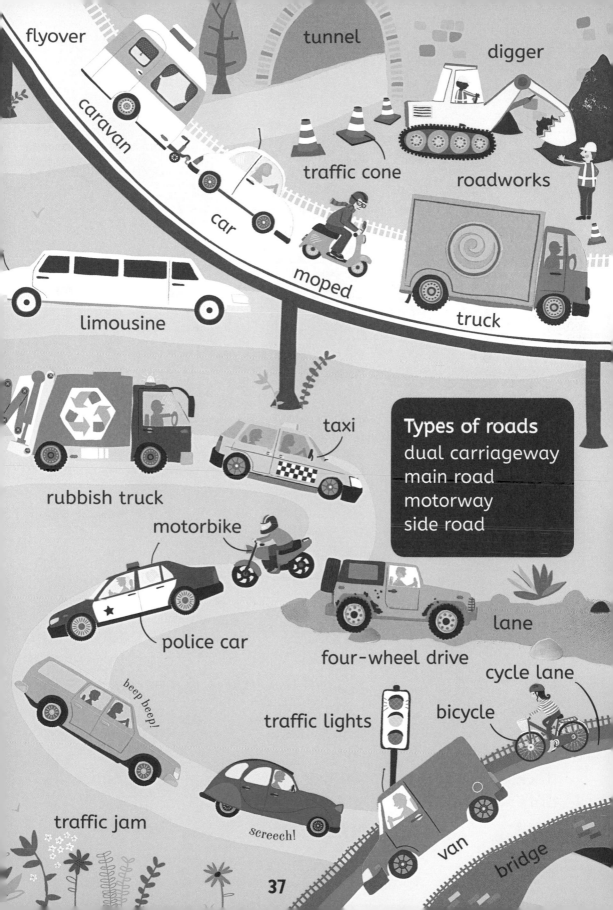

flyover

tunnel

digger

caravan

traffic cone

roadworks

car

moped

truck

limousine

taxi

**Types of roads**
dual carriageway
main road
motorway
side road

rubbish truck

motorbike

police car

four-wheel drive

lane

cycle lane

beep beep!

traffic lights

bicycle

traffic jam

screech!

van

bridge

37

# Ships and boats

bow (front)

container

funnel

stern (back)

anchor

container ship

Land ahoy!

hull

canoe

icebreaker

sail

engine

life jacket

paddle

motorboat

kayak

catamaran

## Ships and boats may ...

bob up and down
capsize
cruise
dock
drift
float

moor
plough through the waves
put to sea
roll
set sail
sink
steam ahead

## On board a ship

captain
cooks
crew
engineers
officers
passengers
sailors
stewards

deck

All aboard!

cruise ship    porthole    lifeboat

bridge

mast

fishing boat

ferry

quay

buoy    tug    barge

Full steam ahead!

rudder

paddle steamer

yacht

oar

rowing boat    narrow boat    lifebelt

# Trains, planes and aircraft

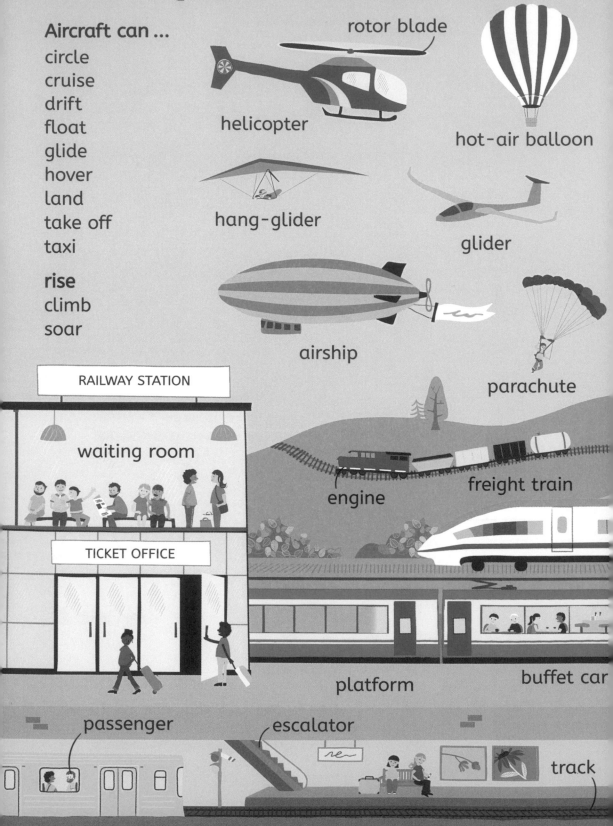

**Aircraft can ...**
circle
cruise
drift
float
glide
hover
land
take off
taxi

**rise**
climb
soar

rotor blade

helicopter

hot-air balloon

hang-glider

glider

airship

parachute

RAILWAY STATION

waiting room

TICKET OFFICE

engine

freight train

platform

buffet car

passenger

escalator

track

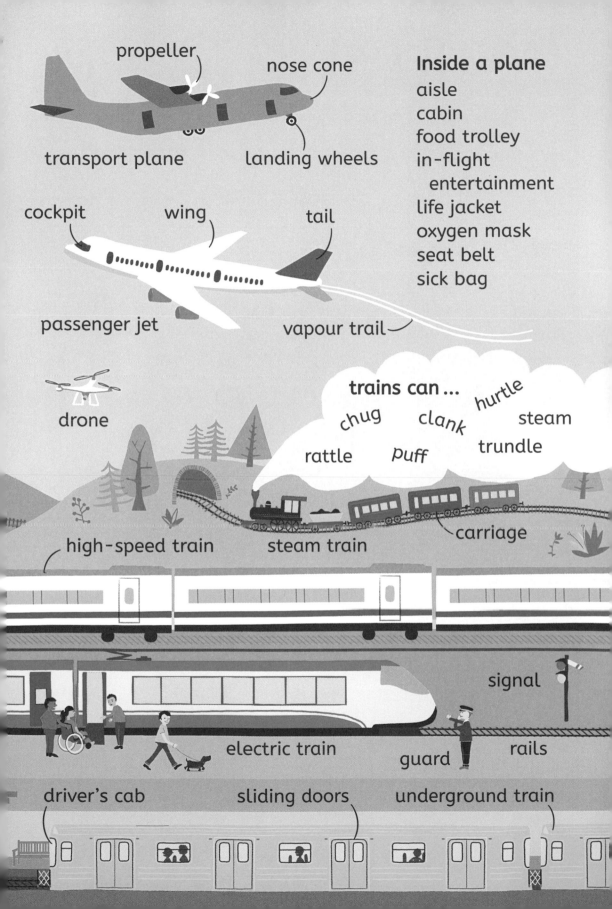

propeller

nose cone

transport plane

landing wheels

**Inside a plane**
aisle
cabin
food trolley
in-flight
  entertainment
life jacket
oxygen mask
seat belt
sick bag

cockpit

wing

tail

passenger jet

vapour trail

drone

**trains can ...**
chug   clank   hurtle   steam
rattle   puff   trundle

high-speed train

steam train

carriage

signal

electric train

guard

rails

driver's cab

sliding doors

underground train

# At an airport

We're going
  on a...
**flight**
journey
trip

**holiday**
break
vacation

**We may feel...**
excited
fidgety
tired
travel-sick

**Flights can be...**
cancelled
delayed
on time
rescheduled

**When do we...**
**leave?**
depart
set off
take off

**arrive?**
land
reach our
  destination
touch down

aeroplane

hangar

shuttle bus

baggage cart

laptop bag

backpack

wheelie case

hand luggage

SECURITY

security
guard

X-ray
machine

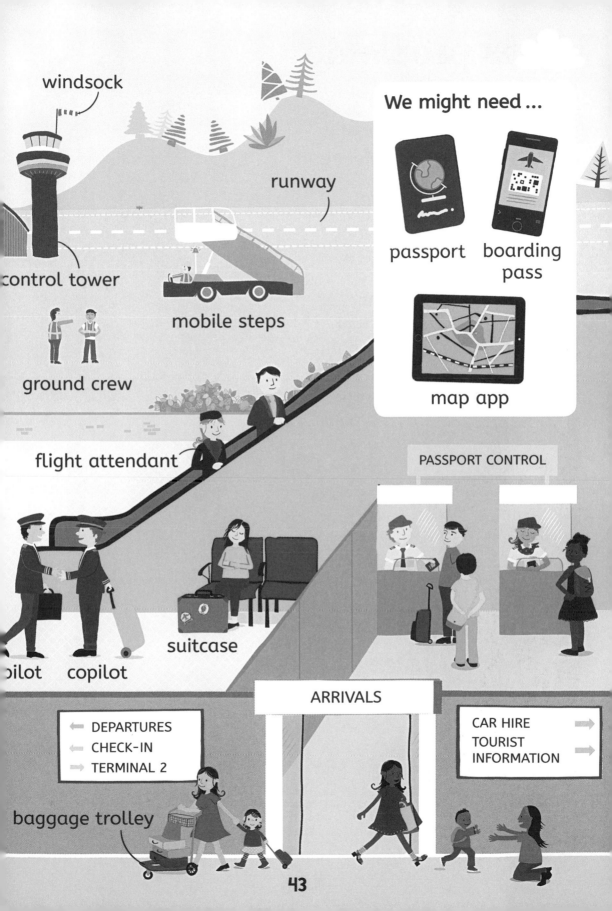

windsock

runway

control tower

mobile steps

ground crew

**We might need ...**

passport

boarding pass

map app

flight attendant

PASSPORT CONTROL

pilot    copilot

suitcase

ARRIVALS

← DEPARTURES
← CHECK-IN
→ TERMINAL 2

CAR HIRE →
TOURIST
INFORMATION →

baggage trolley

43

# Jobs people do

**job**
career
work

**boss**
director
manager
supervisor

**Jobs can be ...**
difficult
easy
enjoyable
exciting
fun
hard
interesting
rewarding
satisfying
tiring

**All sorts
of jobs**
accountant
architect
builder
designer
doctor
electrician
engineer
farmer
journalist
lawyer
librarian
musician
nurse
painter
pharmacist
social worker
teacher

dentist

decorator

chef

police officer

carpenter

hairdresser

plumber

gardener

vet

zookeeper

waiter

receptionist

mechanic

scientist

artist

firefighter

44

# Fun and hobbies

## We like to have fun
enjoy ourselves
have a good time

## fun
enjoyment
entertainment
pleasure

## Hobbies and interests
ballet
chess
computer games
cooking
dancing
drawing
fishing
judo
karate
painting
photography
reading
rollerblading
skateboarding
swimming

## Art equipment
acrylic paints
canvas
chalk
crayons
easel
felt-tip pens
paintbrush
paints
pastels
pencil
rubber
watercolours

## Things to read
atlas
comic
graphic novel
magazine
novel
picture book
reference book
storybook

## Types of stories
adventure story
detective story
fairy tale
ghost story
mystery
science fiction story

## Types of computer
games console
laptop
tablet
PC

## Computer games can be...
amazing
educational
exciting
frustrating
fun
gripping
realistic
superrealistic
time-consuming
violent

## easy
basic
simple
straightforward

## hard
advanced
challenging
complex
complicated
difficult
testing

# Dance and theatre

## Some types of dance
disco dancing
folk dancing
jazz dancing
salsa
tango

line dancing

## Dancers ...
glide
leap
pirouette
spin
stomp
strut
sway
twirl

## Dancers may be ...
dainty
elegant
flexible
graceful
sprightly

tutu
ballerina
ballet

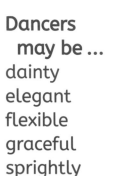
street dancing

tap-dancing

ballroom dancing

| At a theatre you can see a ... | Theatre words | On a set |
|---|---|---|
| ballet | actor | lighting |
| comedy show | cast | props |
| concert | chorus | scenery |
| dance performance | costume | |
| musical | director | **In a theatre** |
| pantomime | interval | aisle |
| play | make-up | balcony |
| puppet show | rehearsal | box |
| talent show | scene | curtain |
| | script | stage |
| | stage manager | stalls |

46

# Film and TV

**Films can be ...**

**exciting**
action-packed
fast-moving
gripping
nail-biting

**boring**
dull
uninteresting
slow-moving
tedious

**funny**
comical
hilarious
ridiculous
side-splitting
whacky

**sad**
depressing
moving
tear-jerking
tragic

**frightening**
creepy
hair-raising
scary
spine-chilling
spooky
terrifying

WOW!  SHHHH!  AARGH!  HA HA HA!

**Films and TV programmes**
cartoon
chat show
comedy
detective series
documentary
drama
game show
horror film
news
science fiction

**Films may include ...**
animation
close-up shots
computer graphics
flashbacks
slow-motion shots
sound effects
special effects
surround sound

**In a cinema, you may hear ...**
coughing
crunching
gasping
giggling
laughing
munching
rustling
slurping
sobbing
whispering

# At a funfair

big dipper

big wheel

ghost train

helter-skelter

carousel

**funfair**
amusement park
fair
theme park

**Fairground
amusements**
big dipper
bouncy castle
bumper cars
hall of mirrors
merry-go-round
simulator
swingboats
teacup ride

**Rides can be ...**
exciting
fast
gentle
nail-biting
scary
thrilling

**On a ride
you may ...**
bounce
lurch
plunge
spin
whirl

**Funfair lights
can be ...**
blazing
colourful
dazzling
flashing
magical

**Funfair music
can be ...**
blaring
booming
deafening
pounding
thumping

# At a circus

tightrope walker

trapeze artists

audience

strongman

clown

ringmaster

acrobats

eek!

## Circus performers may ...
balance on a tightrope
bounce on a trampoline
fly through the air
juggle
ride a unicycle
spin plates
swallow fire
take a bow
walk on stilts
walk on their hands

## Acrobats do ...
backflips
backward rolls
forward rolls
handstands
leaps
somersaults
tumbles
twists

## Clowns may ...
do slapstick routines
mime
throw custard pies

## The audience may ...
cover their eyes
gape
gasp

**applaud**
cheer
clap

**laugh**
cackle
chortle
chuckle
giggle
roar with laughter

# Music words

## Music words
beat
harmony
melody
rhythm
tune

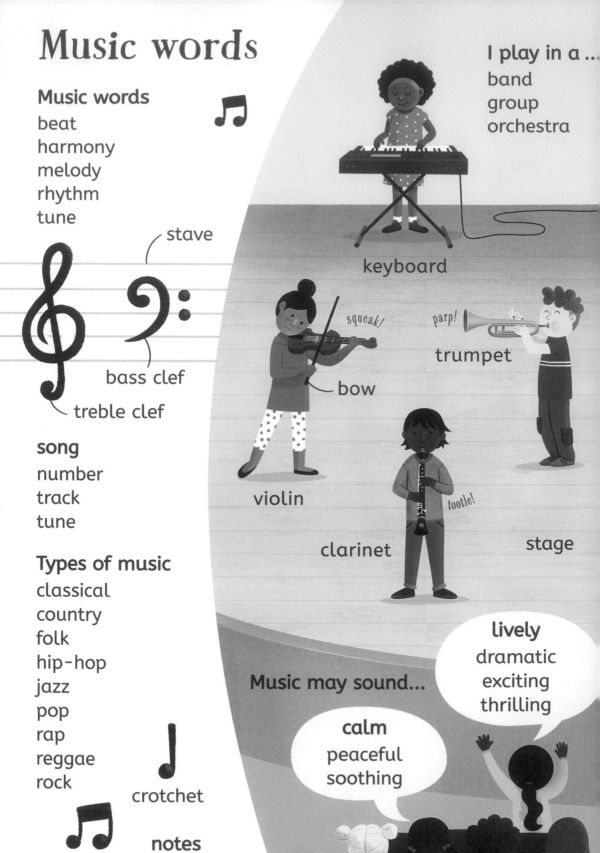

stave

bass clef

treble clef

## song
number
track
tune

## Types of music
classical
country
folk
hip-hop
jazz
pop
rap
reggae
rock

crotchet

notes

quavers

I play in a ...
band
group
orchestra

keyboard

squeak!

parp!

trumpet

bow

violin

tootle!

clarinet

stage

Music may sound...

calm
peaceful
soothing

lively
dramatic
exciting
thrilling

## Musicians may ...

perform
play
practise
rehearse

*clash!* *crash!*

drum kit

## percussion instruments

xylophone

triangle

maracas

cymbals

## Singers may ...

chant
hum
screech
trill
warble

*strum!* *twang!*

guitar

*parp!*

saxophone

microphone

58

lead singer

## More musical instruments

accordion
cello
double bass
electric guitar
flute
harp
organ
piano
recorder
tambourine
trombone

baton

music stand

## Musical equipment

amplifier
speakers
synthesizer

score

conductor

# All sorts of sports

**Types of sports**
athletics
badminton
boxing
fencing
golf
gymnastics
hockey
ice hockey
judo
netball
rounders
rowing
rugby
show jumping
skating
snooker
squash
table tennis
wrestling

skateboarding

baseball

wetsuit

surfing

bow

wicket

arrow

cricket

archery

karate

volleyball

| **Athletics events** | **Sports places** | **Athletes must be ...** |
|---|---|---|
| decathlon | arena | athletic |
| discus | court | determined |
| high jump | field | energetic |
| hurdles | pitch | fit |
| javelin | ring | in great shape |
| long jump | rink | muscular |
| pentathlon | sports hall | skilful |
| pole vault | stadium | speedy |
| sprint | track | strong |

mask

fencing

hoop

basketball

gymnastics

swimming

cycling

tennis

football

## Types of sporting event
challenge
competition
contest
cross-country run
final
game
heat
marathon
match
Olympics
Paralympics
qualifying round
quarterfinal
race
replay
semifinal
time trial
tournament

## Sports moves

**kick**
dribble
pass

**catch**
grab
grasp
snatch
seize

**hit**
drive
knock
putt
slam
strike
swipe at
volley
whack

**throw**
bowl
chuck
fling
hurl
pitch
toss

**dodge**
duck
sidestep
swerve

medal

trophy

# Cats and dogs

**Cats can be ...**
curious
independent
sleek
snuggly
timid

kitten

*purr!*

**meow**
cry
mew

**Cats may ...**
yowl

hiss

scratch

slink

collar

lead

dalmatian

*yelp!*

*woof!*

labrador

greyhound

poodle

dachshund

puppy

**Dogs can be ...**
affectionate
gentle
loyal

**lively**
bouncy
playful

**obedient**
well trained

**disobedient**
mischievous
naughty
wild

**Dogs may ...**
bark
growl
wag their
  tails
whine

# More pets

**Pets may ...**
creep
flutter
slither

**bite**
chew
gnaw
munch
nibble
nip

**jump**
leap
pounce
spring

**run**
scamper
scurry
scuttle
trot

hiss!

tweet!

snake

budgerigar

wheel

hamster

snuffle!

squeak!

rabbit

gerbil

mouse

tank

chameleon

guinea pig

tropical fish

**Pets can look ...**

scaly

furry

fluffy

wiry

# Horses and riding

**Horses may ...**
bolt
buck
canter
gallop
graze
jump
kick
nuzzle
plod
prance
rear
shy
stride
trot
walk

**Horse noises**
clip-clop
neigh
snicker
snort
whinny

**Stable jobs**
changing bedding
cleaning tack
feeding
grooming
mucking out

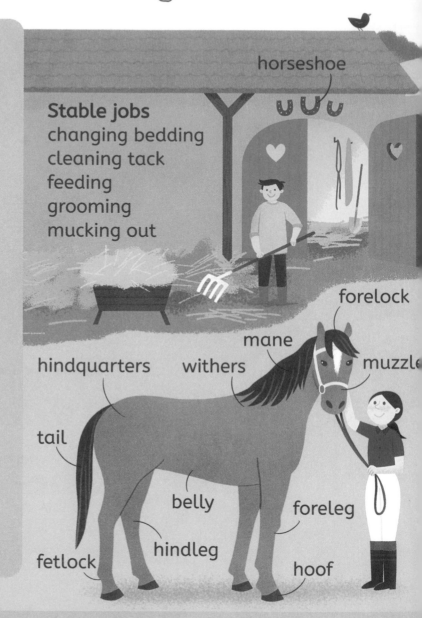

horseshoe

forelock

mane

withers

muzzle

hindquarters

tail

belly

foreleg

hindleg

fetlock

hoof

| Horses may be ... | or they may be ... | horse |
|---|---|---|
| calm | frisky | colt (young male) |
| gentle | highly strung | filly (young female) |
| good-natured | nervous | foal (baby horse) |
| obedient | skittish | mare (female) |
| surefooted | stubborn | pony (small horse) |
| well trained | wild | stallion (male) |

horsebox

jump

## Horses eat ...
apples
carrots
hay
linseed cake
mash
oats
pony nuts

## Riding equipment
crop
harness
leading rein
stable rug

## Riding events
cross-country
dressage
flat racing
gymkhana
hacking
hurdling
point-to-point
pony trekking
showjumping

curry comb

bridle

riding hat

reins

pony

saddle

bit

stirrup

jodhpurs

riding boots

## Types of horse
carthorse
hunter
polo pony
racehorse
show-jumper
thoroughbred

## Horses can look ...
dainty
elegant
glossy
shaggy
sleek
stocky

## Horse colours
bay
chestnut
dapple-grey
grey
palomino
piebald

# Bugs and insects

**insect**
bug
creepy-crawly
minibeast

**Insects may ...**
bite
buzz
crawl
dart
flit
flutter
fly
hover
scurry
scuttle
sting
swarm

beetle

wing

antenna/
feeler

dragonfly

grasshopper

caterpillar

pincer

ladybird

cockroach

earwig

wasp

housefly

butterfly

honeybee

moth

sting

hornet

flea

mosquito

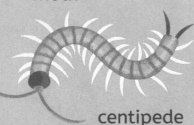
centipede

ant

stick insect

# Animal words

## Some types of animals

mammal

bird

amphibian

insect

reptile

fish

**animal**
creature
beast

**Animal habitats**
desert
grassland
mountain
swamp
woodland

**Animal sounds**
bark
hiss
howl
quack
roar
screech
squawk
squeal

**Animal groups**
a flock of sheep
a herd of cows
a litter of puppies
a pack of wolves
a pod of whales
a pride of lions
a shoal of fish
a swarm of bees

## Males, females and babies

| animal | male | female | baby |
|---|---|---|---|
| chicken → | cockerel → | hen → | chick |
| cow → | bull → | cow → | calf |
| horse → | stallion → | mare → | foal |
| pig → | boar → | sow → | piglet |
| sheep → | ram → | ewe → | lamb |

# Bird words

fly
circle
dart
flap
flit
flutter
glide
hover
sail
soar
swoop

hawk

bluejay

European robin

pheasant

peacock

caw!
beak

crow

egg

chick

nest

canary

wing
feathers
claw

puffin

## More types of birds

bullfinch
cuckoo
dove
emu
falcon
goose
heron
jackdaw
kingfisher
kookaburra

lark
magpie
nightingale
ostrich
raven
sparrow
stork
swallow
thrush
woodpecker

## Bird noises

cackle
call
chatter
cheep
chirp
chirrup
cluck
coo
gobble
hiss

honk
hoot
pipe
quack
screech
sing
squawk
trill
tweet
twitter

coo coo!

pigeon

hummingbird

screech!

blackbird

pelican

HOOT!

seagull

owl

flamingo

quack!

duck

eagle

bird of paradise

**Birds may...**
dive
hop
paddle
peck
perch
plummet
pounce
roost
strut
waddle

**A bird's feathers can look...**
bedraggled
fluffy
ruffled
shiny
smooth

downy

glossy

colourful

speckled

# Trees

acorn

conker

## Trees can be ...
magnificent
spindly
spreading
sturdy

## Tree bark can be ...
gnarled
papery
ridged
rough
smooth

## Types of trees
ash
beech
birch
elm
hawthorn
hazel
horse chestnut
larch
magnolia
mahogany
maple
monkey puzzle

oak
olive
palm
plane
poplar
rowan
rubber
sweet chestnut
sycamore
walnut
weeping willow
yew

## Evergreen trees

branch

cone

pine      spruce      cedar      holly      redwood

## Fruit trees

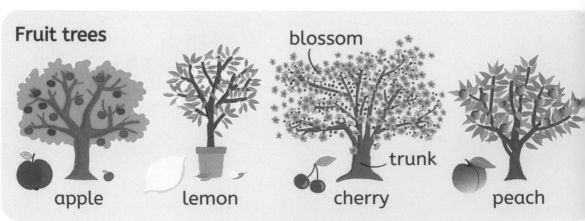

blossom

trunk

apple      lemon      cherry      peach

# Bushes and flowers

## Types of flowers
carnation
cowslip
daffodil
daisy
dandelion
forget-me-not
hollyhock
hyacinth
marigold
orchid
primrose
snowdrop
violet
wallflower
waterlily

## Types of bushes
bramble
currant
gorse
laurel
lavender
lilac
privet
rosemary
thyme

## Bushes can be...
bushy
clipped
overgrown
prickly

## Flowers can be ...
beautiful
colourful
delicate
spectacular
straggly
sweet-smelling

buttercup

pansy

iris

rose

poppy

bud

sweet pea

leaf

seeds

petal

lily

crocus

tulip

foxglove

stalk

sunflower

bluebell

# In the country

**field**
meadow
pasture

**path**
lane
track
trail

**hill**
hillside
mound

**wood**
forest
woodland

**Countryside words**
barn
bog
cottage
fence
gate
grass
hedgerow
lake
pond
pool
scarecrow
village

**In the country you may spot a...**
badger
hare
hedgehog
mole
rabbit
squirrel

field

fox

stile

wild flowers

deer

**Woods can be...**
dark
filled with
 dappled sunlight
gloomy
shadowy
spooky

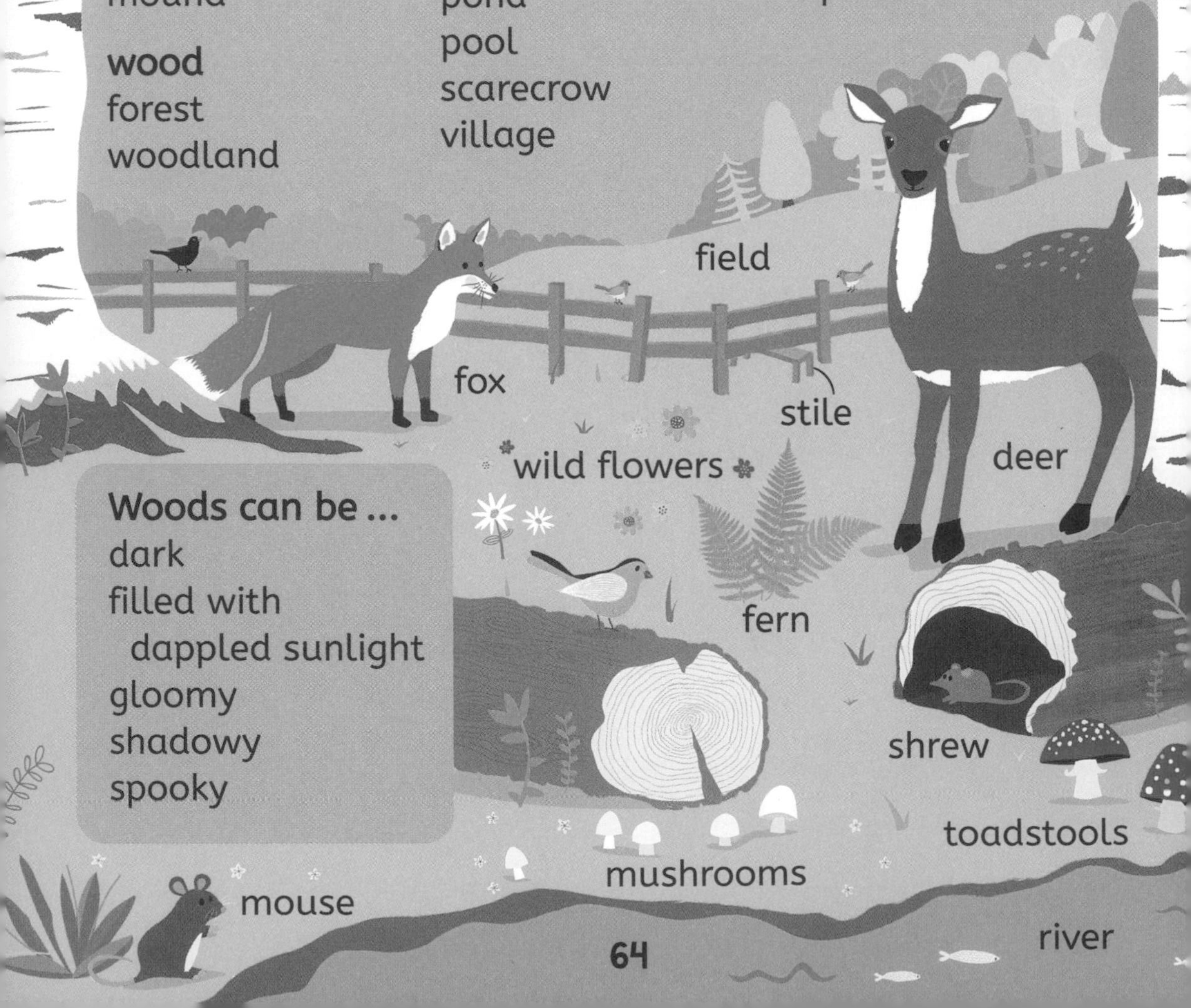

fern

shrew

mushrooms

mouse

toadstools

river

64

# On a farm

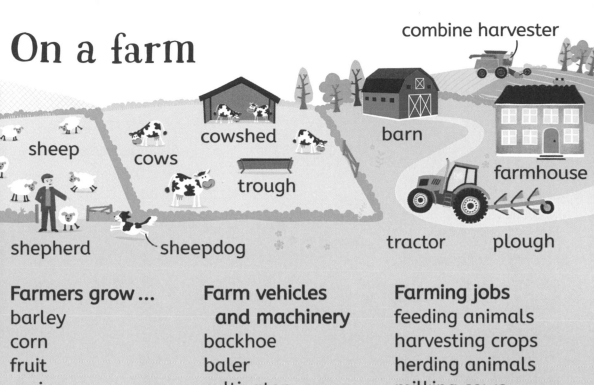

combine harvester

sheep

cows

cowshed

trough

barn

farmhouse

shepherd

sheepdog

tractor

plough

## Farmers grow ...
barley
corn
fruit
maize
oats
oilseed rape
sugar beet
vegetables
wheat

## Some farm animals
donkey
goat
goose
pig

## Farm vehicles and machinery
backhoe
baler
cultivator
loader
milking machine
mower
muck-spreader
seed drill
roller
trailer

## Farming words
hay
manure
straw

## Farming jobs
feeding animals
harvesting crops
herding animals
milking cows
picking fruit
planting vegetables
ploughing
rounding up sheep
shearing sheep
sowing seeds
spraying
weeding

henhouse

turkey

duck

cockerel

hen

eggs

ducklings

65

chicks

# Rivers, lakes and ponds

**river**
brook
creek
stream
torrent

**Rivers may be ...**
choked with weeds
crystal clear
deep
fast-flowing
murky
polluted
shallow
sluggish
sparkling
stagnant

**Rivers may ...**
babble
break their banks
bubble
burble
cascade
flood
flow
froth
murmur
pour
splash
surge
swirl
trickle
twist
wind

**Along a river
you might see ...**
gorge (deep valley)
island
lock
towpath
weir

**Lake and river
sports**
fishing
kayaking
sailing
swimming
water-skiing
whitewater
rafting

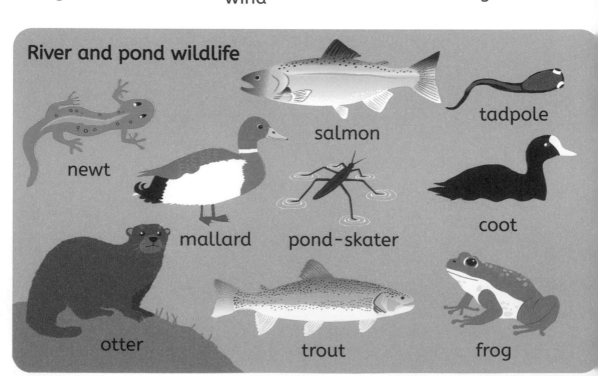

## River and pond wildlife

newt

salmon

tadpole

mallard

pond-skater

coot

otter

trout

frog

bridge

rapids

yacht

lake

jetty

river bank

waterfall

stepping stones

mooring quay

rowing boat

damselfly

kingfisher

heron

moorhen

toad

pond/pool

reeds

pondweed

frogspawn

waterlily pad

**67**

# In the mountains

**Mountains can be ...**
high
lofty
snow-capped
soaring
towering

**Their slopes can be ...**
craggy
forested
icy
rocky
steep

**More mountain words**
avalanche
black ice
glacier
snowstorm

**top**
peak
summit

chairlift

whoosh!

ski run

snowboarder

**bottom**
base
foot

snowmobile

Wheee!

**toboggan**
sled
sledge

husky sledge

fir trees

frozen lake

cable cars

climbing
rope

ice axe

slope

slalom
course

drag lift
button lift
T-bar

ledge

nursery slope

chalet

SKATE HIRE

skating rink

cross-country skiers

## Mountain sports can be ...
challenging
dangerous
exciting
risky

## Climbers ...
clamber
cling onto the
  rock face
lose their
  footing
reach the summit
scramble
tumble

## Skiers and snowboarders ...
jump
perform tricks
race
speed
swerve

## Skaters ...
balance
fall
glide
twirl
wobble

# In a desert

palm trees

vulture

camel train

sand dune

oryx

skull

oasis

water hole

cactus

camel

jerboa

cobra

dung beetle

scorpion

**Deserts are often ...**
dry
sandy
scorching

**but some are ...**
freezing
rocky
stony

**The sun is ...**
blazing
blinding
dazzling

**You may be ...**
parched
sunburned/sunburnt
sweaty

**Some desert animals**
desert fox
desert rat
lizard
locust
rattlesnake
tarantula

# In a jungle

canopy
(tree tops)

butterfly

toucan

tree frog

screech!

spider monkey

vine

parrot

creeper

orchid

sloth

swamp

jaguar

army ants

| Jungles can be... | Jungle trees and plants... | Some jungle animals |
|---|---|---|
| dark | coil | armadillo |
| gloomy | dangle | chimpanzee |
| humid | loop | gorilla |
| lush | scratch | orangutan |
| noisy | snake | python |
| steamy | sting | tapir |
| swampy | tower | tiger |

# Grassland animals

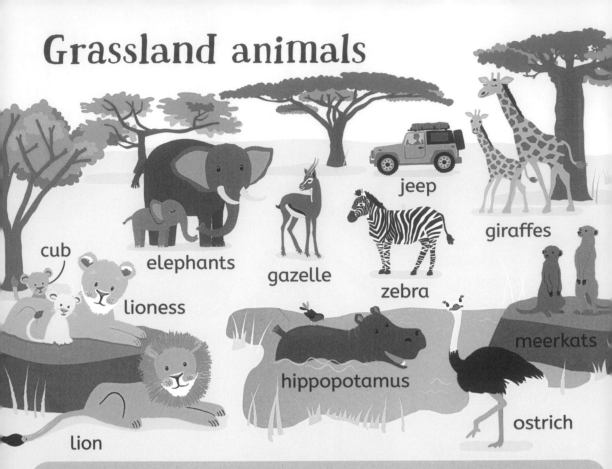

cub

elephants

gazelle

jeep

giraffes

zebra

lioness

meerkats

hippopotamus

lion

ostrich

**Animals roam the grasslands ...**
plains
savanna

**Some grassland animals**
antelope
buffalo
cheetah
crocodile
hyena
leopard
rhinoceros
warthog

**The animals may ...**
attack
charge
hide in the undergrowth
hunt
lie in wait
lurk in the bushes
pounce
prowl
snap their jaws
stalk their prey
thunder over the plain

**You may hear a ...**
bellow
crash
crunch
growl
grunt
hiss
howl
roar
rustle
screech
snap
snarl
splash
squeal

# Under the sea

**Fish and sea creatures**
dolphin
eel
lobster
porpoise
pufferfish
seahorse
sea lion
sea snake
seal
squid
swordfish
whale

**Fish may ...**
crest the waves
dart
dive
drift
float
glide
leap out of the water
lurk
plunge
splash
surface
swim

**Under the sea it can be ...**
beautiful
cold
colourful
dark
mysterious
scary
silent

**sea**
ocean

**sea bed**
ocean floor

parrotfish

octopus

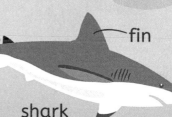
fin

shark

turtle

shoal of fish

oxygen tank

mask

scuba diver

angelfish

clownfish

coral reef

ray

73

# At the seaside

## At the seaside you may see...
caves
cliffs
pier
rock pools
sand dunes

## A seaside resort may be...
crowded
deserted
empty
packed
peaceful
picturesque
quiet
sleepy
touristy

## Beaches may be...
pebbly
sandy
stony

## Things to take to the beach
beach ball
bucket and spade
flippers
folding chair
picnic
snorkel
suncream
sunglasses
sunhat
swimsuit
towel
wetsuit

## Seaside activities
building sandcastles
collecting shells
paddling
playing mini-golf
sailing
scuba diving
snorkelling
sunbathing
surfing
swimming
water-skiing

## Sea words
high tide
low tide
spray
surf
white horses

hotel
souvenir shops
ice-cream van
caravan
windbreak
kite
volleyball
jetty
surfer
kitesurfer
surfboard

# Sea and shore

**sea**
ocean

**beach**
coast
sands
shingle
shore

**The sea may be ...**
calm
choppy
crystal clear
glassy
green
grey
raging
rough
shimmering
sparkling

**The waves may ...**
billow
break
churn
crash
foam
lap
pound
race
roar
roll
surge
swell

**In a rock pool**
anemone
barnacle
sea urchin
shrimp

## Nature at the beach

driftwood

gull

crab

jellyfish

starfish

shells

cormorant

seaweed

promenade

campsite

beach café

lifeguard

parasol

pedalo

windsurfer

rubber dinghy

fishing net

# Words for weather

Today, the weather is ...

**hot**
baking
blistering
boiling
roasting

scorching
sizzling
sweltering
tropical

**cold**
bitter
bracing
chilly
cool

freezing
nippy
perishing
wintry

**cloudy**
gloomy
grey
miserable
overcast
dreary
dull

**fine**
dry
mild
sunny
warm

**rainy**
damp
drizzly
showery
spitting
wet

**windy**
blowy
blustery
breezy
gusty
stormy

weather vane

**foggy**
hazy
misty
murky
smoggy

**steamy**
clammy
close
humid
muggy

F° C°

thermomete

## Types of windy weather

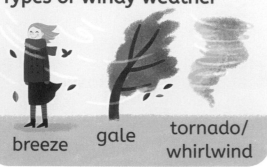

breeze

gale

tornado/
whirlwind

## Types of wet weather

hail

shower

sleet

downpour

# Ice, frost and snow

icicle

**Snow may...**

melt    thaw

fall

swirl

drift    float    settle

## Ice can be ...
brittle
cracked
glassy
hard
slippery
smooth

## Snow can be ...
crisp
crunchy
dazzling
deep
powdery
slushy

## Frost may ...
glisten
glitter
sparkle

## The ground may be ...
as hard as iron
blanketed with snow
carpeted with snow
dusted with snow
frozen solid
sprinkled with snow

## The trees may be ...
bare
covered with frost
laden with snow
weighed down by snow

## In the snow you ...
plod
plough through
sink in
struggle
stumble

## On the ice you ...
glide
skate
skid
slide
slip

snowflake

## More ice, frost and snow words
avalanche
Jack Frost
snowball
snowdrift

snowman

sledge    snow angel

# Storm words

**storm**
blizzard
hurricane
monsoon
snowstorm
thunderstorm
typhoon

**Thunder ...**
booms
cracks
echoes
growls
roars
rolls
rumbles

**Lightning ...**
flares
flashes
lights up the sky
strikes
zigzags

**Rain ...**
beats down
buckets down
lashes down
pelts down
pours down
teems down
tips down

**Storms can be ...**
awesome
deafening
destructive
devastating
dramatic
ear-splitting
frightening
powerful
raging
savage
terrifying
violent
wild

hailstones

forked
lightning

**Storms may ...**
block roads
bring down
  power lines
cut off villages
damage crops
destroy buildings
flood homes
swell rivers
uproot trees

**More storm
  words**
billowing clouds
inky sky
thunderbolt
thunderclap
thundercloud

The wind ...

gusts

shrieks

howls

blasts

rages

blows

# Night words

crescent moon

## The night may be ...
clear
moonlit
shadowy
starlit

## The sky may be ...
inky
pitch-black
starry
velvety

## Night-time sounds
bats sqeaking
cats yowling
clocks chiming
doors slamming
floorboards
  creaking
owls hooting
people snoring
sirens wailing
windows banging

## At night, it can feel ...
ghostly
gloomy
hushed
peaceful
scary
silent
spooky
still

## Times of night
dawn
daybreak
dusk
midnight
nightfall
the small hours

## Some night-time animals
badger
glow-worm
hedgehog
nightingale

## The moon may be ...
bright
hazy
hidden behind
  a cloud
pale
silvery
waning (growing
  smaller)
waxing (growing
  larger)

## The stars may ...
flicker
glimmer
glitter
shimmer
shine
sparkle
twinkle

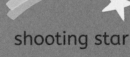
shooting star

fireflies

owl

moths

bat

# Fire and fireworks

**Fireworks...**
blaze
dazzle
explode
fizzle out
flare
shoot
shower
sink
soar
sparkle
spin
spiral
whizz
whoosh
zoom

**Fireworks can be...**
dazzling
deafening
magical
spectacular
stunning

**Firework sounds**
boom
splutter
whine
whistle

**Types of firework**
banger
Catherine wheel
firecracker
fountain
rocket
Roman candle
sparkler

*pop!*
*crash!*
*fizz!*
*hiss!*
*crackle!*
*squeal!*
*bang!*
*screech!*

**Fires...**
blaze
burn
glow
rage
roar
scorch
smoulder

**Smoke...**
billows
chokes
curls
drifts
envelops
swirls

**Flames...**
dance
flare
flicker
glow

# Noisy words

## Stop that noise!
din
hullabaloo
racket
rumpus

## Bells ring
chime
clang
jingle
peal

*ding-dong!*

## Doors bang
crash
slam
thud

## People shout
bellow
call out
roar
yell

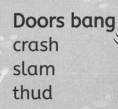

## Children scream
screech
shriek
squeal

## Dancers stamp
clatter
clomp
stomp

## Fountains splash
babble
glug
gurgle

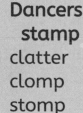

*splosh!*

## Drums boom
roll
thunder
rumble

*squeak!*

| loud | quiet | deep | high |
|------|-------|------|------|
| deafening | hushed | booming | high-pitched |
| ear-splitting | muffled | low | piercing |
| noisy | soft | low-pitched | shrill |

# Fairy-tale words

magic
enchantment
sorcery
witchcraft
wizardry

witch

fairy godmother

leprechaun

princess

giant

Fee fi
fo fum

fairy

dragon

prince

king    queen

goblin

pixie

unicorn

gnome

toadstool

horse and carriage

elf

| Fairy-tale characters may... | The good characters are... | The bad characters are... |
| --- | --- | --- |
| cast spells | beautiful | creepy |
| change shape | brave | cunning |
| come to the rescue | generous | evil |
| fight battles | gentle | menacing |
| grant wishes | handsome | sinister |
| solve riddles | kind | ugly |
| vanish into thin air | pretty | wicked |

**giant**
hulk
ogre

**wizard**
magician
sorcerer

**cast a spell**
bewitch
enchant
transform

**Wizards and witches use a...**
cloak of invisibility
crystal ball
flying broomstick
magic potion
magic wand

**Wizards say...**
Abracadabra!
Hocus pocus!
Shazam!

**Fairy-tale places**
castle
cave
cavern
cottage
dungeon
forest
lake
maze
palace
tower
tunnel
wood

Hey presto!

**spell**
charm
curse

bat

book of spells

199 Top Spells

zap!

cauldron

wizard

Magic potions...
boil
bubble
simmer
fizz
froth

**Potion ingredients**
bat's wing
dragon's blood
snake's tongue
unicorn's horn

# Pirates and treasure

**Pirates can be ...**
bloodthirsty
bold
brutal
cruel
daring
fearless
fierce
greedy
menacing
reckless
swashbuckling

**Pirates may ...**
board ships
bury treasure
explore desert
  islands
fire cannons
force prisoners to
  walk the plank
go ashore
keep a lookout
scrub the deck
sing sea shanties
take prisoners

**steal**
loot
plunder
raid
rob

Shiver me timbers!

lookout

telescope

Jolly Roger/skull and crossbones

sail

Yo ho ho!

figurehead

plank

cabin boy

cannon

anchor

message in a bottle

**Pirate ships may ...**
brave the storm
cross the ocean
ride the waves
run aground

**In a storm, a ship may ...**
groan
shudder
sink/capsize

mast

crow's nest

captain

rigging

shark-infested
waters

eye patch

hook

goblet
chalice
cup

chest
casket
trunk

peg leg
wooden leg

crown
coronet
tiara

cutlass

gold coins

**treasure**
booty
bounty
loot
riches

**jewels**
gems
precious stones

**coins**
ducats
doubloons
pieces of eight

**Types of
   jewellery**
bangles
beads
bracelets
brooches
earrings
necklaces
rings

**Precious stones**
amber
amethyst
diamond
emerald
pearl
ruby
sapphire
turquoise

**Treasure can be ...**
dazzling
gleaming
glittering
inlaid with gems
sparkling

**Or it can be ...**
dusty
grimy
rusty
tarnished
worthless

# In space

constellation

helmet

life-support pack

satellite

galaxy

comet

spacesuit

astronaut

space station

**spaceship**
rocket
spacecraft

**Other spacecraft**
moon buggy
spacelab
space shuttle

**Other space words**
Milky Way
universe

**Spaceships may ...**
blast off
crash land
cruise
lift off
orbit the Earth
re-enter the
  Earth's
  atmosphere
zoom through
  space

**Astronauts may ...**
contact mission
  control
conduct
  experiments
experience
  zero gravity
float
hover
moonwalk
spacewalk

asteroid belt

**Solar system**

Sun

Moon

Uranus

Mercury

Earth

Jupiter

Neptune

Venus

Mars

Saturn

**planets**

# On a space adventure

flying saucer

volcano

dust storm

gas cloud

zoom!

whoosh!

zap!

laser gun

alien

rocket

crater

**You might travel by...**
starship
teleporter

**You might meet...**
androids
extraterrestrial
  beings
Martians
shape shifters
space pirates

**You might be...**
caught in an
  intergalactic war
lost in deep space
stranded on a
  distant planet
stuck in a
  parallel universe
sucked into a
  black hole
trapped in a force
  field

**Planets may be...**
airless
baking
barren
dusty
frozen
glowing
icy
rocky
teeming with life
uninhabited
windy

# Ghosts and haunted houses

**Ghostly sounds**
bang
bump
clank
clatter
clink
crash
creak
groan
hammer
knock
moan
mutter
rattle
screech
sigh
sob
thud

cackle!

cape

full moon

broomstick

witch

cobweb

bats

spider

zombie

coffin    vampire

skeleton

tombstone

**Ghostly sounds can be...**
bloodcurdling
chilling
creepy
eerie
hair-raising
heart-stopping
spine-chilling
weird

**Ghosts may...**
appear
beckon
drift
float
glide
haunt
hover
vanish
waft

**You may...**
be rooted to
  the spot
be scared out
  of your wits
cover your eyes
hide
run for your life
scream
shudder

**ghost**
ghoul
gremlin
poltergeist
spirit

*wail!*

*creak!*

**Haunted houses
can be...**
creepy
crumbling
dark
deserted
gloomy
menacing
moonlit
mysterious
neglected
rambling
shadowy
spooky

*howl!*

*yowl!*

black cat

mist

werewolf

**In a haunted house**

| | | |
|---|---|---|
| attic | oak chest | **You may see or hear...** |
| cellar | panelled room | banging windows |
| dungeon | secret passageway | clanking chains |
| family portraits | spiral staircase | creaking |
| four-poster bed | stone steps | floorboards |
| grandfather clock | suit of armour | fluttering curtains |
| library | tower | guttering candles |
| locked door | trap door | hidden laughter |
| looking glass | turret | muffled screams |

# Monsters

**Monsters may be ...**
curious
fire-breathing
friendly
greedy
one-eyed
slimy
smelly
spiteful

**fierce**
bloodthirsty
ferocious
rough
savage
violent

**ugly**
hideous
monstrous

**Monster homes**
bog
castle
cave
dungeon
forest
lake
swamp
well

Monsters may have ...

wrinkles

tangled hair

warts

spikes

scales

hairy toes

fiery breath

shaggy fur

webbed feet

Monsters may ...
belch    bellow
grumble    roar

slime

tentacles

# Dinosaurs

## Types of dinosaurs
brachiosaurus
diplodocus
iguanodon
stegosaurus
velociraptor

## Dinosaurs may have ...
bony plates
leathery wings
pointed fangs
scaly skin

## Dinosaurs may ...
attack
charge
chase
chomp
fight
hunt
kick
munch
pounce
rear up
snarl
snatch

## Large dinosaurs may ...
lumber
plod
thunder

## Small dinosaurs may ...
gallop
scamper
scuttle
trot

beak

pterosaur

lava

## Volcanoes ...
erupt
rumble
send out
  clouds of ash
smoke
smoulder

club tail

roar!

ankylosaurus

claws

horn

ferns

tyrannosaurus

triceratops

# Adventure words

**Some places for adventures**

haunted mansion

pyramid

cave

desert island

hidden chamber

lost city

castle

tunnel

temple

**Castles may be ...**
awe-inspiring
crumbling
gloomy
magnificent
ruined

**Lost cities may be ...**
abandoned
deserted
empty
forgotten

**Caves may be ...**
damp
echoing
freezing
icy cold
pitch-black

**Cave walls may be ...**
dripping
gleaming
glistening
slimy
slippery

**Hidden chambers may be ...**
airless
cramped
dark
musty
shadowy
stuffy

**Tunnels may be ...**
narrow
twisting
winding

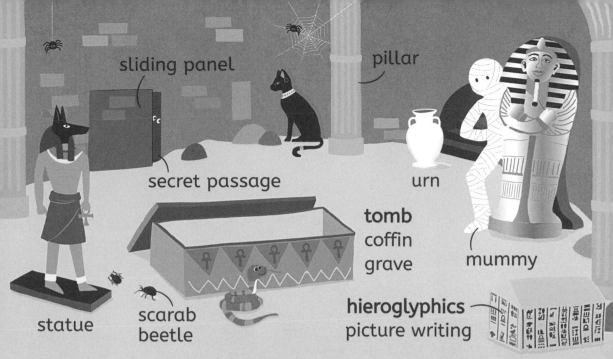

sliding panel

pillar

secret passage

urn

tomb
coffin
grave

mummy

statue

scarab
beetle

hieroglyphics
picture writing

## Adventures may be ...

action-packed
amazing
dangerous
exciting
frightening
incredible
spine-chilling
terrifying
thrilling

## Some adventure clues

chart
coded message
diary
inscription
manuscript
map
photograph
sealed letter
secret code

## You will need to be ...

adventurous
brave
curious
daring
determined
inquisitive

treasure
chest

## You may need ...

STAY SAFE!

survival kit

compass

rope ladder

camera

codebook

binoculars

notebook

torch

penknife

# Knights and castles

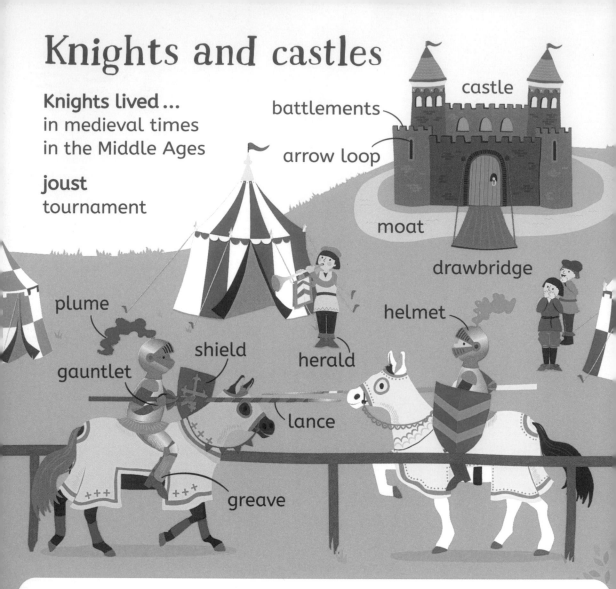

**Knights lived ...**
in medieval times
in the Middle Ages

**joust**
tournament

battlements

castle

arrow loop

moat

drawbridge

plume

helmet

gauntlet

shield

herald

lance

greave

**Places in a castle**
bedchamber
chapel
courtyard
dungeon
gatehouse
great hall
keep (central
  fortress)
kitchen
watchtower

**Knights wore ...**
chainmail
a suit of armour

**Knights' weapons**
battle-axe
broadsword
dagger
morning star
  (spiked ball
  on a chain)

**Battle weapons
  and equipment**
arrows
battering ram
boiling oil
catapult
crossbow
longbow
pikestaff
siege tower
slingshot

# At a feast

feast
banquet

coats of arms

tapestry

piper
fiddler

minstrels' gallery

page
lord
lady
high table

goblet
platter

jester
fool

acrobat
juggler
dancer

| Food at a feast | Guests at a feast | Lords and ladies wore ... |
|---|---|---|
| boar's head | bishop | cloak/mantle |
| boiled custard | king | coronet |
| jellied eels | knight | fur-lined gown |
| marzipan swan | noble | headdress |
| pastry castle | priest | hood |
| pigeon pie | prince | robe/dress |
| roast heron | princess | tights/hose |
| roast peacock | queen | tunic |
| salted fish | sheriff | veil |
| venison | squire | |

# Word finder

Do you want to find an alternative for a particular word? This word finder will show you where to find other interesting words to use in its place.

## a

afraid
see **scared**, 17

amazed
see **surprised**, 16

amazing
see **nice**, 6

**angry**, 16

**announce**, 14

annoyed
see **grumpy**, 17

**answer**, 14

anxious
see **worried**, 16

**applaud**, 49

**arrive**, 42

**ask**, 14

astonished
see **surprised**, 16

attractive
see **good-looking**, 10

## b

**bad**, 6

bad-tempered
see **grumpy**, 17

**bang** (door), 81

**beach**, 75

beautiful
see **good-looking**, 10
see **nice**, 6

beg see **ask**, 14

**big**, 7

**bite**, 55

**blue**, 8

boastful
see **proud**, 19

boiling
see **hot**, 76

**bored**, 16

**boring**, 47

**bottom**
(mountain), 68

bouncy
see **lively**, 19

brainy
see **clever**, 19

**brave**, 19

**bright** (colour), 8

brilliant
see **bright**, 8
see **good**, 6

**build**, 30

**busy** (city), 32

## c

calm
(person) 18
(music) 50

car
(types), 36, 37

**carry**, 15

**catch**, 53

chat
see **talk**, 14

**cheap**, 34

cheeky
  see **naughty**, 19
  see **rude**, 18

cheer
  see **applaud**, 49

**cheerful**, 18

**chest**
  (treasure), 85

chew
  see **bite**, 55
  see **eat**, 26

**chop**
  (food), 27

clap
  see **applaud**, 49

**clean** (house), 29

**clear**
  (see-through),
  31

**clever**, 19

**climb**, 15

**cloudy**, 76

**clumsy**, 19

**cold**
  (food and
    drink), 25
  (weather), 76

comment
  see **mention**, 14

conceited
  see **proud**, 19

concentrate on
  see **think about**,
  14

**confident**, 19

**confused**, 16

**cook**, 27

cool
  see **cold**, 76

crash
  see **bang**, 81

**crazy**, 18

creepy
  see **frightening**,
  47

cross
  see **angry**, 16
  see **grumpy**, 17

crowded
  see **busy**, 32

**crown**, 85

cruel
  see **unkind**, 18

**cry**, 17

curious
  see **nosy**, 19

# d

daring
  see **brave**, 19

**dark**
  (colour), 8

deceitful
  see **dishonest**, 18

decide
  see **think
    about**, 14

**deep**
  (sound), 81

**delicious**, 26

deliver
  see **give**, 15

depressed
  see **sad**, 16

depressing
  see **sad**, 47

deserted
  see **empty**, 32

difficult
  see **hard**, 45

**dirty**
  (city), 32
  (clothes), 13

**disgusting**, 26

**good**, 6

**good-looking**, 10

grab
  see **catch**, 53
  see **hold**, 15
  see **take**, 15

grave
  see **tomb**, 93

great
  see **nice**, 6

**green**, 8

**grey**, 8

grin
  see **smile**, 17

**grumpy**, 17

guess
  see **think**, 14

gurgle
  see **splash**, 81

# h

hand over
  see **give**, 15

handsome
  see **good-
    looking**, 10

**happy**, 16

**hard**
  (material), 31
  (game), 45

**hate**, 17

**healthy**, 18

**hear**, 21

heavy
  see **big**, 7

help yourself
  see **take**, 15

helpful
  see **nice**, 6

**high**
  (sound), 81

hilarious
  see **funny**,
    19, 47

**hill**, 64

**hit**, 53

**hold**, 15

**holiday**, 42

**honest**, 18

horrible
  see **bad**, 6

**hot**
  (food and
    drink), 25
  (weather), 76

huge
  see **big**, 7

hurt
  see **upset**, 17

# i

imagine
  see **think**, 14

important
  (decision)
    see **big**, 7

inquisitive
  see **nosy**, 19

intelligent
  see **clever**, 19

invent
  see **think up**, 14

irritable
  see **grumpy**, 17

# j

**jewels**, 85

jingle
  see **ring**, 81

jolly
  see **cheerful**, 18

**jump**, 15

a b c d e f g h i j k l m n o p q r s t u v w x y z

A B C D E F G H I J K L M N O P Q R S T U V W X Y Z

**naughty**, 19

neat
see **smart**, 13

**nervous**, 18

**nice**, 6

**noise**, 81

noisy
see **loud**, 81

**nosy**, 19

notice
see **feel**, 21
see **hear**, 21
see **see**, 21
see **taste**, 21

## o

**obedient** (dog), 54

**old**, 18

**orange**, 8

## p

pale
see **light**, 8

**path**, 64

**pattern** (types), 9

peaceful
see **calm**, 18, 50

peak
see **top**, 68

pick
see **take**, 15

place
see **put**, 15

**pink**, 8

point out
see **mention**, 14

**pointed**, 9

**polite**, 18

press
see **push**, 15

pretty
see **good-looking**, 10

**proud**, 19

**pull**, 15

**purple**, 8

**push**, 15

**put**, 15

puzzled
see **confused**, 16

## q

**quickly**, 26

**quiet**, 81

## r

**rainy**, 76

recover
see **get better**, 23

**red**, 8

**refreshing**, 25

relaxed
see **calm**, 18

reply
see **answer**, 14

revolting
see **bad**, 6

ridiculous
see **funny**, 19, 47

**ring** (bell), 81

roar
see **shout**, 81

rob see **steal**, 84

rough
see **fierce**, 90

A B C D E F G H I J K L M N O P Q R S T U V W X Y Z

**round** (shape), 9

**rude**, 18

**run**, 15

## S

**sad**
(feeling), 16
(film), 47

**say**, 14

**scared**, 17

scary
see **frightening**, 47

**scream**, 81

**scruffy**, 13

**see**, 21

see-through
see **clear**, 31

**sensible**, 19

serious (decision)
see **big**, 7

**shabby**
(building), 32
(clothes)
see **scruffy**, 13

sharp
see **pointed**, 9

**shiny**, 32

shocked
see **surprised**, 16

**shop** (types), 34

**short**, 7

**shout**, 81

**shy**, 19

silly
see **crazy**, 18

simple
see **easy**, 45

**sit**, 15

skinny
see **thin**, 7

slam
see **bang**, 81

sled
see **toboggan**, 68

sleepy
see **tired**, 17

slice
see **chop**, 27

slim
see **thin**, 7

**slowly**, 26

**small**, 7

**smart**
(clothes), 13
see **clever**, 19

**smell**, 21

**smile**, 17

**smooth**
(material), 31

snatch
see **take**, 15

snobbish
see **proud**, 19

snooty
see **proud**, 19

**soft**
(material), 31
(sound)
see **quiet**, 81

solid
see **hard**, 31

**song**, 50

sparkling
see **shiny**, 32

**spell** (magic), 83

spiteful
see **unkind**, 18

**splash**, 81

**squash**, 15

squeal
  see **scream**, 81

squeeze
  see **squash**, 15

**stamp**, 81

stand
  see **put**, 15

**steal**, 84

**steamy**, 76

**storm**, 78

**story** (types), 45

**strong**
  (person), 18
  (material), 31

stuck-up
  see **proud**, 19

stunning
  see **nice**, 6

sunny
  see **fine**, 76

suppose
  see **think**, 14

**surprised**, 16

swerve
  see **dodge**, 53

# t

**talk**, 14

**talk loudly**, 14

**talk quietly**, 14

**take**, 15

take care of
  see **look after**, 23

**tall**, 7

**taste**, 21

tense
  see **nervous**, 18
  see **worried**, 16

terrified
  see **scared**, 17

terrifying
  see **frightening**, 47

**thick**
  (hair), 11

**thin**
  (hair), 11
  (person), 7

**think**, 14

**think about**, 14

**think up**, 14

thrilled
  see **excited**, 16

**throw**, 53

**tidy**, 29

**tight** (clothes), 13

**tiny**, 7

**tired**, 17

**toboggan**, 68

**tomb**, 93

**top**
  (mountain), 68

touch
  see **feel**, 21

tough
  see **strong**, 31

**treasure**, 85

truthful
  see **honest**, 18

try
  see **taste**, 21

tug
  see **pull**, 15

# u

**ugly**, 90

unhappy
  see **sad**, 16

a b c d e f g h i j k l m n o p q r **s** **t** u v w x y z

A B C D E F G H I J K L M N O P Q R S T U V W X Y Z

unimportant
(mistake)
see **small**, 7

unkind, 18

untidy
see **messy**, 29

upset, 17

# V

vain
see **proud**, 19

vast
see **big**, 7

**vegetable**
(types), 25

violent
see **fierce**, 90

**violet**, 8

# W

**walk**, 15

wander
see **walk**, 15

**warm**
(food and
drink), 25

watch
see **look**, 21

**weak**
(person), 18
(material), 31
(weather), see
**fine**, 76

well
see **healthy**, 18

weep
see **cry**, 17

whisper
see **talk quietly**,
14

wicked
see **bad**, 6

wide
see **big**, 7

wild
see **naughty**, 19

**windy**, 76

**wizard**, 83

wonder
see **think**, 14

wonderful
see **nice**, 6

**wood**
(forest), 64

work
see **job**, 44

work out
see **think about**,
14

worn out
see **tired**, 17

**worried**, 16

# Y

yell
see **shout**, 81

**yellow**, 8

**young**, 18